Welcome! This book will take you deeper into Victorian Modern Cursive handwriting.
But fill in your licence before you dive in!
Diving Licence
Name:
Address:
Date of birth:
Where do you want to go diving?
What equipment will you need?
What are you hoping to find?
Draw a picture of yourself in your diving gear.
AF584376

Progressive improvement check

Write the sentence below in joined writing. Rate your writing, then ask your teacher to rate it.

Quick sharks swiftly snaffled the dozy divers from the rocks, chomping them like toffee.

Term 1 Date ____________

My rating:

Teacher's rating:

Term 2 Date ____________

My rating:

Teacher's rating:

Term 3 Date ____________

My rating:

Teacher's rating:

Term 4 Date ____________ (Use speed loops.)

My rating:

Teacher's rating:

☆ Revision – Letter families

Trace and copy.

The i family

l t i j

Clockwise letters

m n r x z

Other clockwise letters

h p k

Anti-clockwise letters

a c d g q

Other anti-clockwise letters

o e f s

The u family

u y v w b

Write all the body only letters.

Write all the head and body letters.

Write all the body and tail letters.

Which letter has a head, body and tail? Write this letter 6 times.

Colour the top wedges green and the bottom wedges red. Copy each letter.

a d m n g h

k p q r u w

☆ Revision – Diagonal joins

A diagonal join goes from one letter's exit UP to meet the next letter.

Trace and copy.

an dr em ev hi in kn

li nu pr sn tu un xe

drip pink mine knew

nut exit silly under

creep empty every keep

enemy hymn chimney

Trace then copy these words with diagonal joins to and from s.

hands cakes use snow

☆ Revision – Diagonal joins to f

Trace and copy these letter pairs with diagonal joins to f.

lf uf af if ef nf pf hf

Trace and copy these words with diagonal joins to f.

shelf tuft fifty leapfrog

after beef mouthful fifth

self Assessment

Rate your diagonal joins to f.

Needs work | Good effort | Best ever!

Trace, then copy.

oy ou on oi op or ow

ri rn rp rv ry vi vy

wi wn wr bi br fi fr

Now trace these words.

some trip burn opal

visit win wry bite

fix fur fright fun

☆ Revision – Horizontal joins to e

The letter e starts halfway between the lines.

Remember to dip down when making a horizontal join to e.

dip down to join

oe re ve we be ve

Trace then copy to practise these joins to e.

oe re ve we be oe re we

Trace and copy these words.

goes whoever volcanoes

before forehead lyrebird

deceive allowed weather

beast better benefit

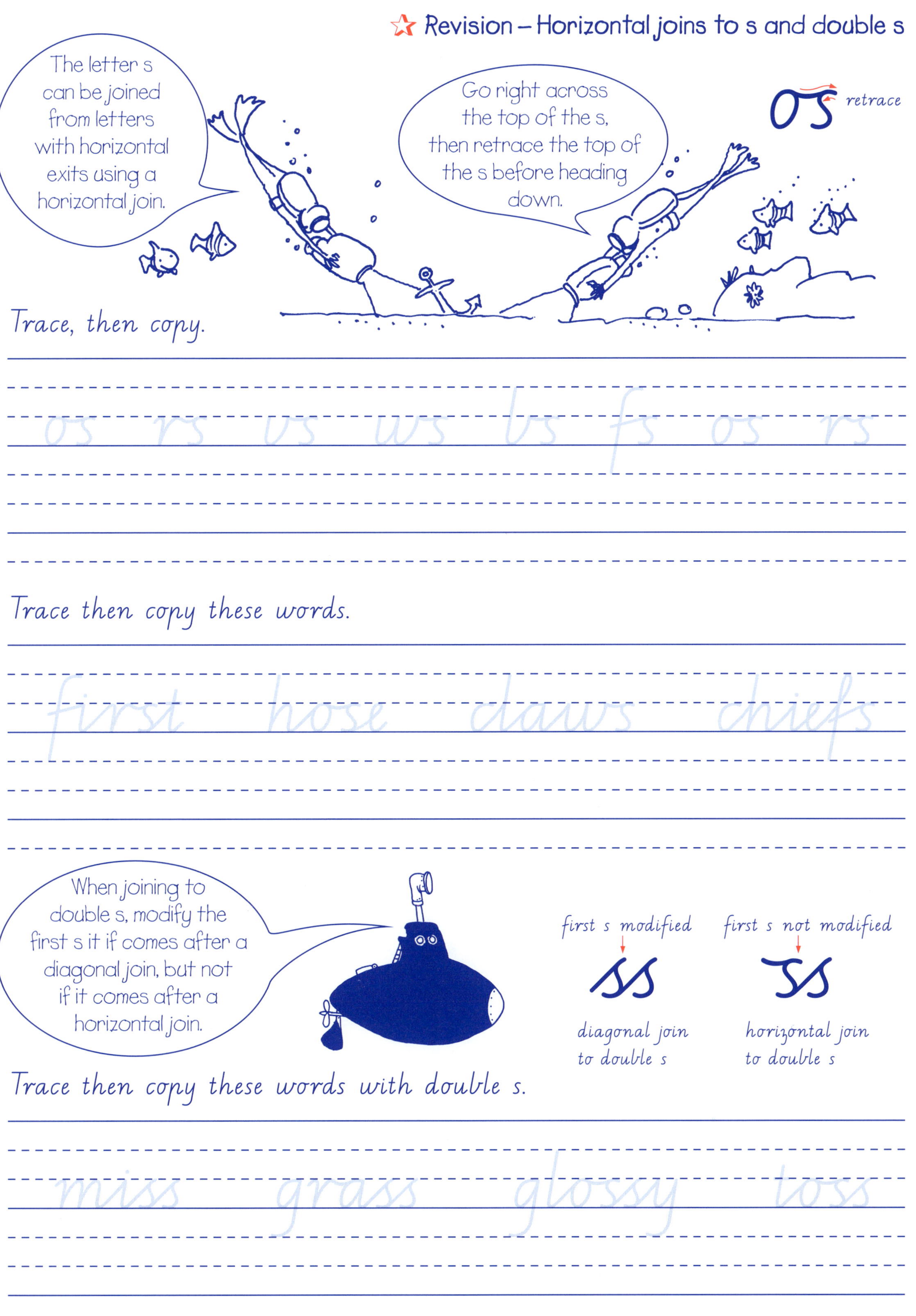

Trace, then copy.

os rs vs ws bs fs os rs

Trace then copy these words.

first hose claws chiefs

Trace then copy these words with double s.

miss grass glossy toss

☆ Revision – Horizontal joins to f and from f

Trace and copy these words with horizontal joins to f.

roof turf awful clubfoot

Trace and copy these words.

fly flow fetch fearful

☆ Revision – Diagonal and horizontal joins to o

Trace, then copy.

no po to co do ho lo

motor solo tomato snow

Trace, then copy.

bo ro oo vo wo fo ro

bottle room voice woman

☆ Revision – Touch joins

Trace, then copy. Then choose four letter pairs, and put a star * to show where you lifted your pencil.

ea ia ha ac ec ed id

eg ig aq eq ca ud ng

Copy these words. Change colour when you lift your pencil to do a touch join. The marks ˅ will help you.

mammal echinoderm

Write these words so there are no gaps in the touch joins.

gadget quads sing

When you join to a, c, d, g or q, lift your pencil. Don't retrace!

lift pencil here

wa

start again here

Trace, then copy.

oa oc od og oq oc ocean

ra rc rd rg rq ra racing

va va vc vd va vacuum

wa wd wc wa wd crowd

ba bc bd bg ba baked

fa fa fa fabric fastener

Revision – Diagonal joins to ascenders

When you join to a head and body letter, remember to retrace on your way back down.

To make sure you retrace carefully, pause at the magic line on your way up.

l not l

Trace, then copy.

ab at ch ck nl nk dl

hl lb ll th ub ul kl

mb ml eb el ik il nl

Copy, taking care when retracing the downward strokes of the tall letters.

Yellow butter melts quickly.

Is there salt in the salad?

Go from the horizontal join right to the top of the head and body letter. Then retrace a little as you come back down.

For careful retracing, pause at the magic line and at the top of the letter.

magic line — pause — pause — retrace

r → r → rl

Trace and copy.

ol ol ol rl rk rl rb

wh wk wl bl bt bb fl

Trace. Underline the horizontal joins to head and body letters.

When it's hot, going
surfing helps me to cool off.
I was pretty awkward
when I started surfing, but
I got better with lots of
extra practice.

☆ Revision – Letters that don't join

These letters don't join to the letter after them.

g j y z

Copy these letter pairs. Then trace and copy the words.

ja jam je jeep ji jinx

jo joke ju just ja jab

ga gave ge get gi gifts

go ago gu gush gr grow

ye yes yi yippee yo your

za zany ze zebra zi zipper

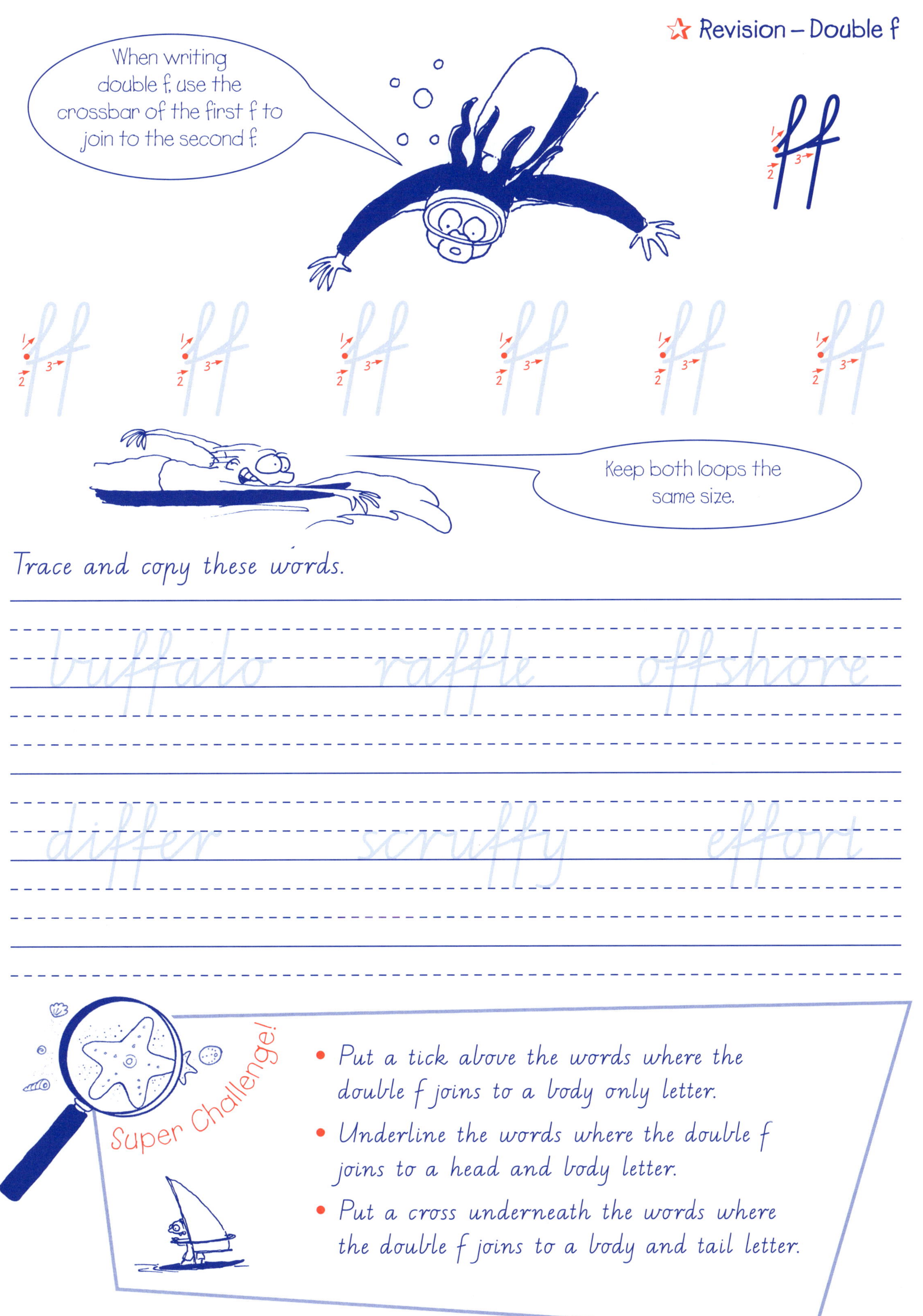

Trace and copy these words.

buffalo raffle offshore

differ scruffy effort

Super Challenge!

- Put a tick above the words where the double f joins to a body only letter.
- Underline the words where the double f joins to a head and body letter.
- Put a cross underneath the words where the double f joins to a body and tail letter.

Super Challenge!

- Circle the double letters that have a diagonal join.
- Underline the double letters that have a horizontal join.
- Put a tick above the double letters that have a touch join.
- Put a cross underneath the double letters that don't join.

Now copy the letter pairs.

bb cc dd ee gg ll nn pp

rr ss tt mm aa oo ii uu

Trace and copy these words with double letters.

seaweed aggressive nibble

ruffle paddling shallow

Rewrite these island names in joined writing.

Rottnest Barrow

Kangaroo One Tree

Baffin Great Keppel

Tollgate Possession

Look at these letter pairs:

mp or al so fi ac ws

if wh ff of vo es be

★ Circle the letter pairs that would make diagonal joins.

★ Underline the letter pairs that would make horizontal joins.

★ Put a box around the letter pairs that would have touch joins.

Now write the letter pairs in joined writing.

Write this sentence in joined writing. Then put a mark ˅ above the touch joins. Underline any diagonal joins to head and body letters.

Anchovies really taste good!

Circle any letter pairs that don't join. Write the sentence in joined writing.

Some people just get oysters.

Teacher

Copy.

Maritime archaeologists and
marine biologists do a lot of diving
in the course of their work. Other
people have jobs that involve diving
too, including police divers, marine
park rangers and Navy Seals.

Copy this list of great diving sites around the world.

Great Barrier Reef, Australia

Sharm-el-Sheikh, Red Sea, Egypt

Sulawesi, Indonesia

Madang, Papua New Guinea

Monterey Bay, California, U.S.

Antarctic Peninsula, Antarctica

self Assessment

Look at the letters in each word.
Are they spaced evenly?
Rate your letter spacing.

Uneven spacing —— Even spacing

Rewrite this passage, using even spaces between the words.

Make the spaces between words as even in size as you can. When words are too close together or too far apart, writing can be difficult to read. When words are spaced evenly, writing is easier to read.

Copy. Make the spacing between words as even as you can.

Drift netting involves suspending

a strong plastic net between two

buoys. The net catches anything

that swims into it, including

dolphins and turtles.

Write one argument against the use of drift netting.

Circle the word with the most even letter spacing.

snorkeller snorkeller snorkeller

Rewrite these words with even letter spacing.

from hoop for provide were

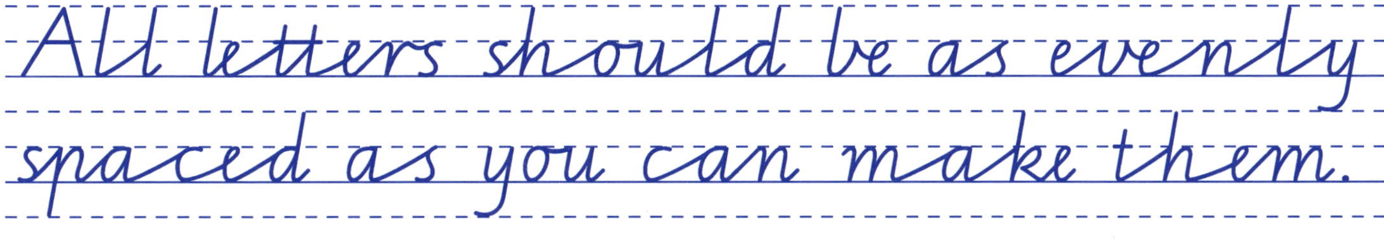

Rewrite these words with even letter spacing.

All letters should be as evenly spaced as you can make them.

Rewrite this passage, spacing the letters within the words evenly.

Port Lincoln in South Australia is
Australia's major tuna fishing and
processing centre. In Australia,
tuna are fished by pole or long
line. This means that the stocks
of other fish aren't harmed.

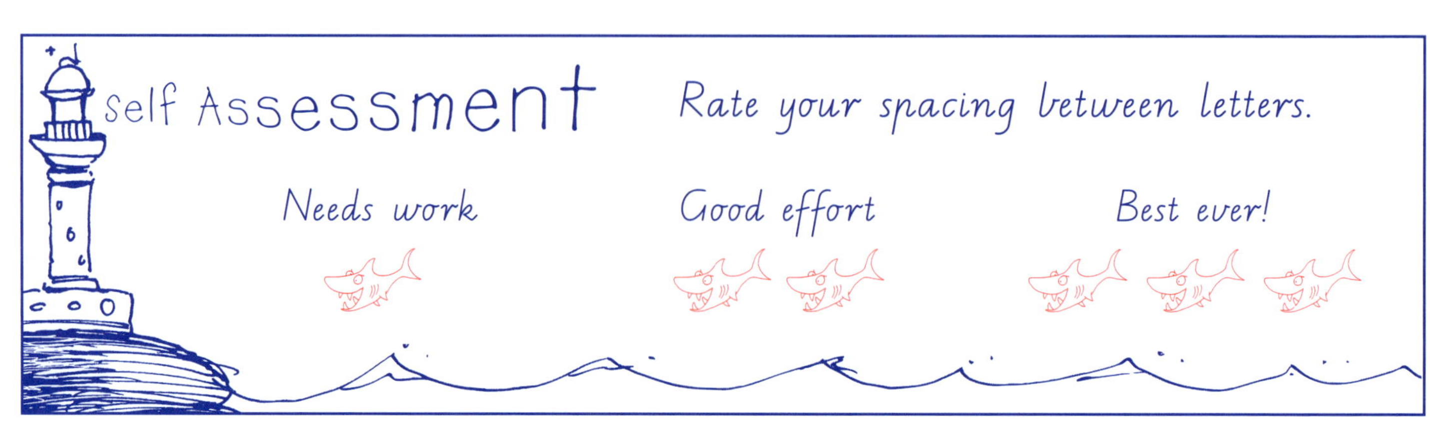

Assessment page – Letter size and spacing, space between words

Look carefully at the passage below, then:

- ★ circle any letters that are not the right size
- ★ put a cross under words where the letters are not evenly spaced
- ★ underline pairs of words that are not evenly spaced.

Rewrite this passage correctly.

When Australia had penal
colonies, convicts came to Australia
by ship. The triptook months an d
conditions were ve ry bad. After
World war two, many people
migrate d to Australia by ship.

Teacher

Trace.

a b c d e f g h i j k l m

n o p q r s t u v w x y z

Trace and copy these words in print script.

prawns mackerel cod snapper

flounder eel zebra fish tuna

Use an atlas to research the oceans of the world. Use print script to label the five main oceans.

Arctic Southern Pacific

Atlantic Indian

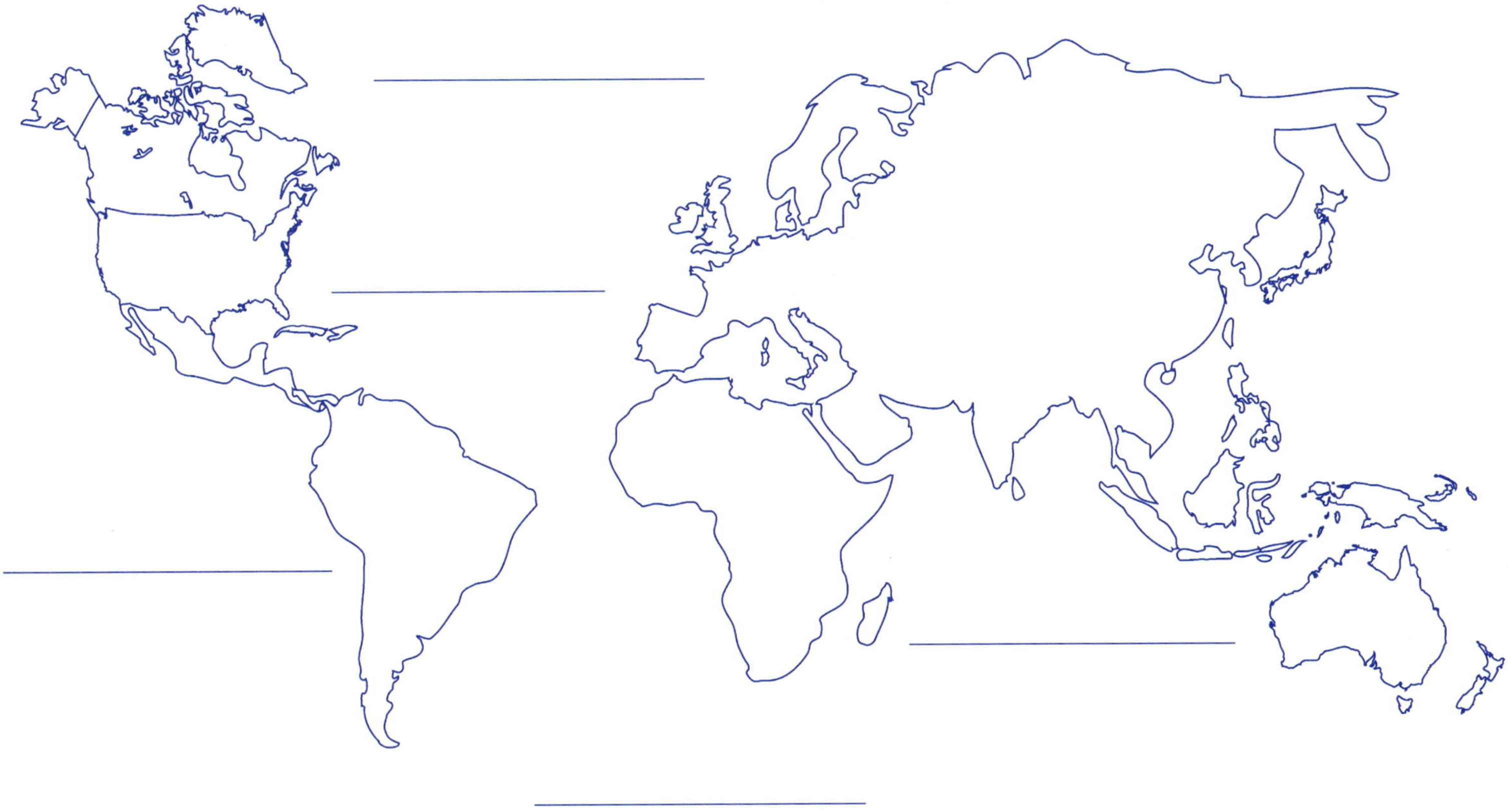

Self Assessment

Rate your print script.

Needs work | Good effort | Best ever!

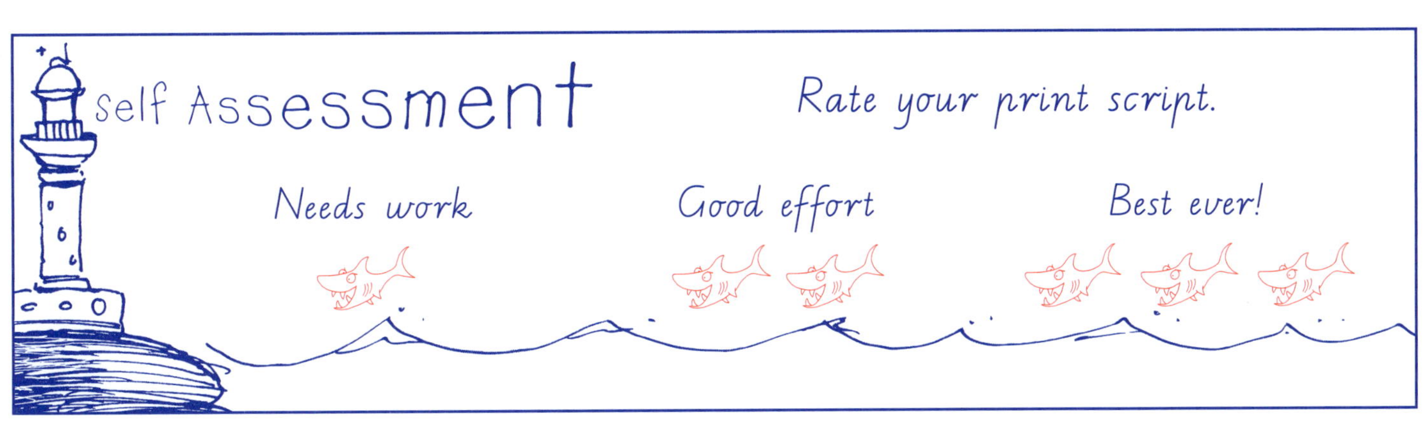

Use these words to label the shark, using print script.

pectoral fin snout gill slits

caudal fin nostril anal fin

dorsal fin eye mouth pelvic fin

Trace the words at the bottom of the page. Then use them to label the picture. Remember to print.

1. ______________
2. ______________
3. ______________
4. ______________
5. ______________
6. ______________
7. ______________
8. ______________
9. ______________
10. ______________
11. ______________

1. mask 2. hood 3. air tank 4. dive computer 5. knife 6. fins 7. wet suit 8. weight belt 9. buoyancy control jacket 10. torch 11. regulator

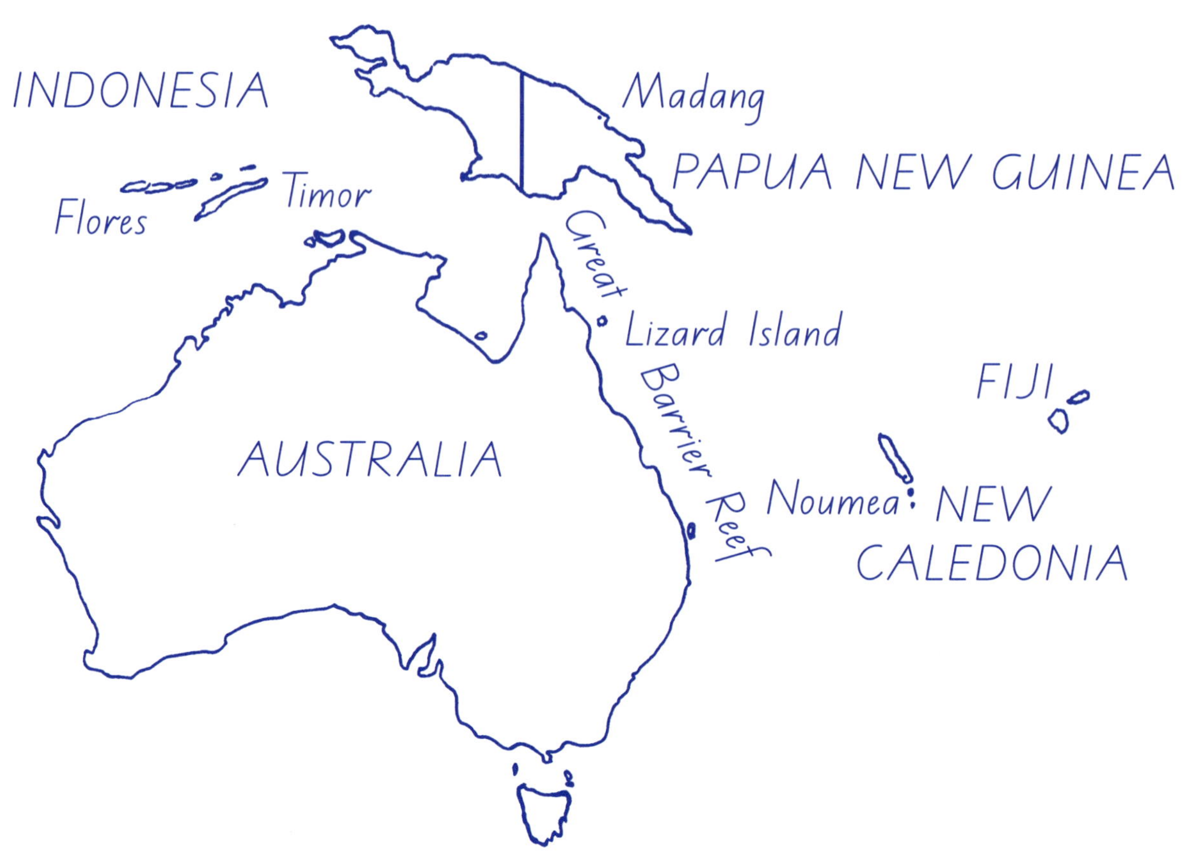

Label this map using print script, so it matches the map above.

Write the alphabet in print script.

Label the ocean animals using print script.

octopus tuna weedy sea dragon
shark angler fish

Teacher

Copy.

Squid, cuttlefish, octopuses and

nautiluses all belong to the group of

animals called "cephalopods". All

cephalopods except for the nautilus

have eight arms with suckers or

hooks. They can be found in

shallow reefs as well as the deep sea.

Copy.

As well as having eight arms,

squid and cuttlefish have a set of

feeding tentacles. Cephalopods can

propel themselves through the water

at great speeds by jetting water out

of their siphons.

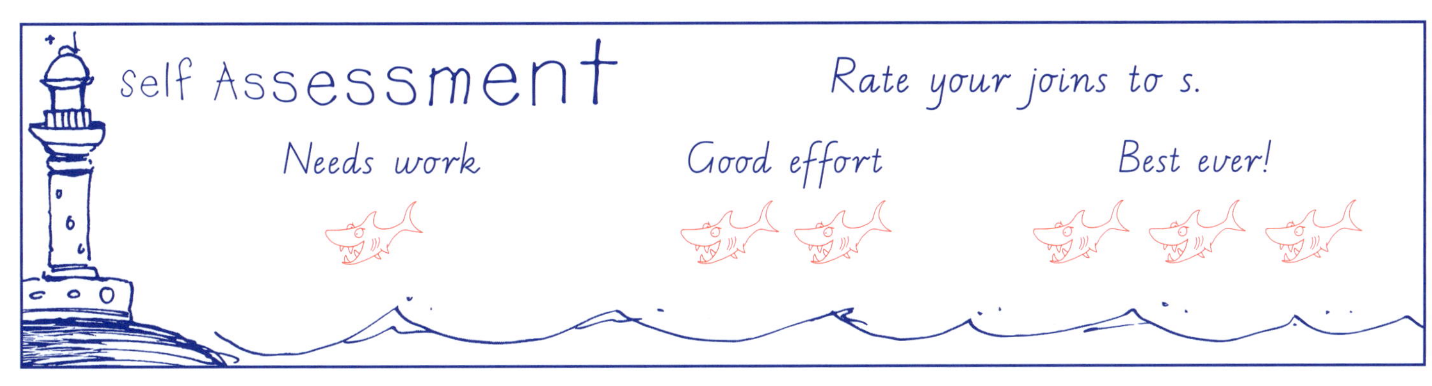

Copy.

The ocean is an amazing place. It is home to many wonderful plants and animals. Some are colourful, some are highly intelligent, some are dangerous and some are quite bizarre. Humans have been in awe of the sea for centuries.

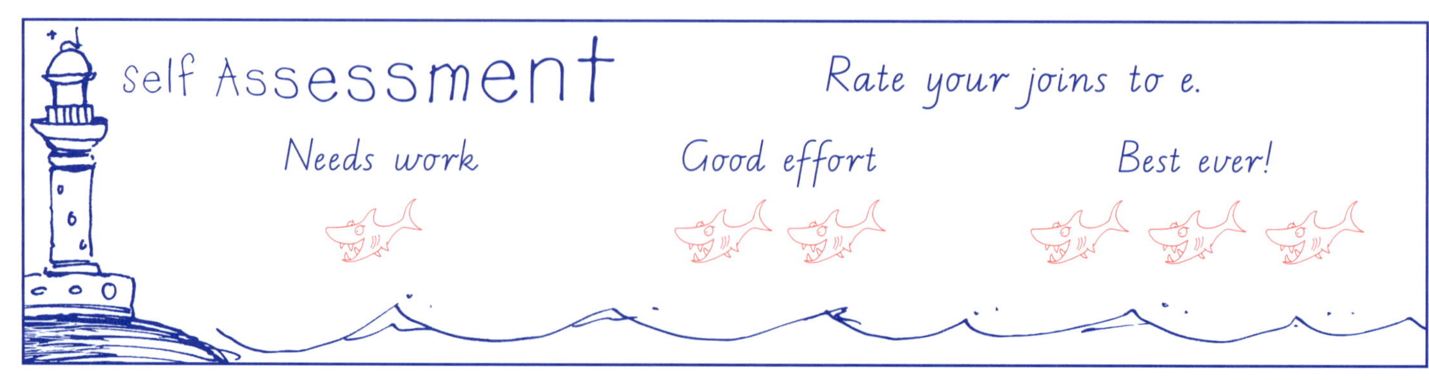

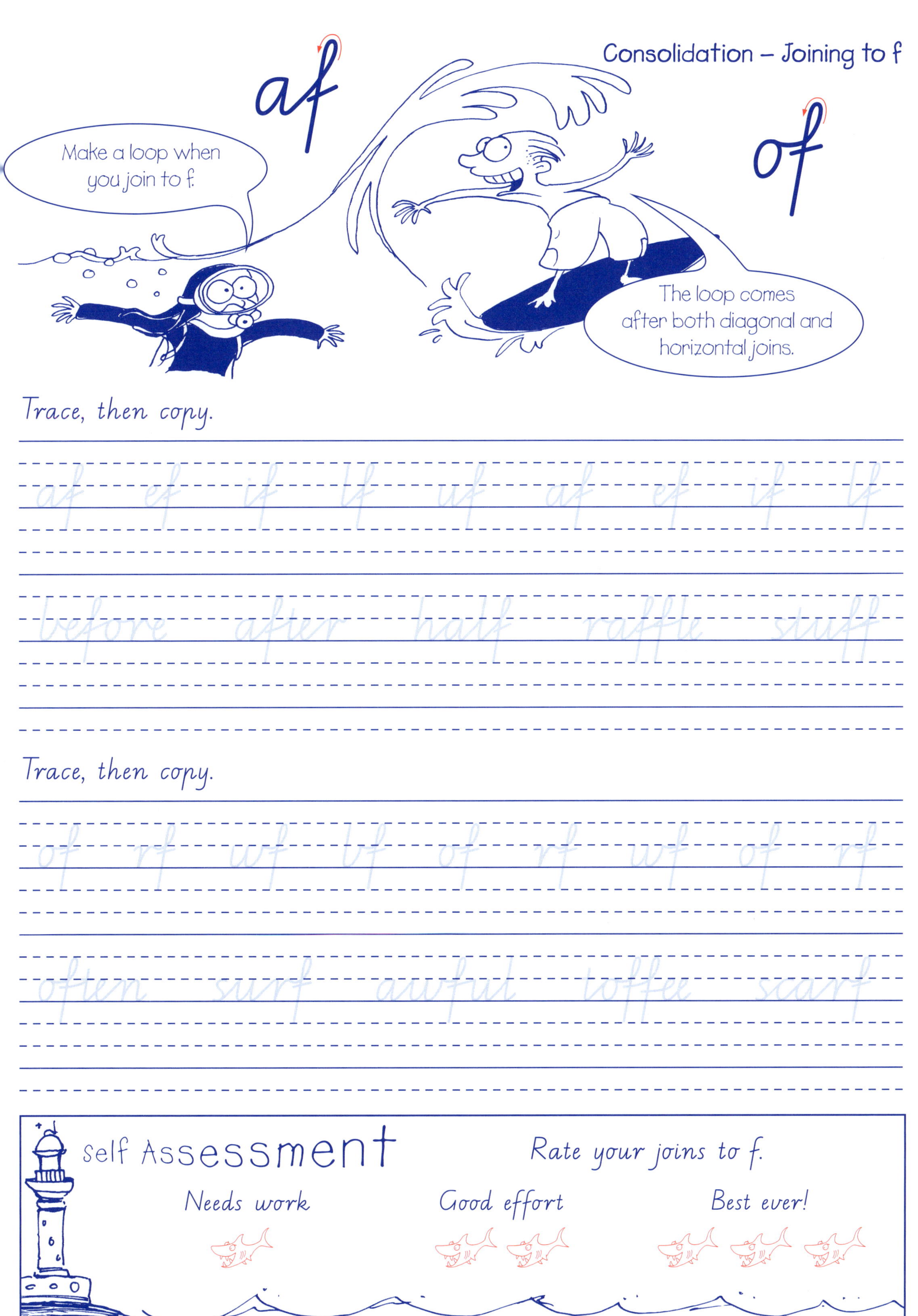

Trace, then copy.

af ef if lf uf af ef if lf

before after half raffle stuff

Trace, then copy.

of rf wf bf of rf wf of rf

often surf awful toffee scarf

self Assessment

Rate your joins to f.

Needs work

Good effort

Best ever!

Copy this list of ocean sports. Then add a mark ˅ to show any touch joins. The first one has been done for you.

kayaking canoeing parasailing

paragliding snorkelling

scuba diving wave skiing

boogie boarding wind surfing

Practice these touch joins.

ha ic ed og aq rd ba ig wd

self Assessment

Rate your touch joins.

Needs work

Good effort

Best ever!

Copy.

Tankers are huge vessels that carry

liquid cargo such as petroleum and

natural gas to ports all over the

world. When accidents happen,

tankers sometimes spill huge

amounts of oil into the sea.

- Underline 3 horizontal joins to e.
- Put a mark ˅ above 5 touch joins.
- Tick 5 diagonal joins to head and body letters.
- Draw a box around 3 letter pairs that do not join.

Underline the letters that do not join, then copy.

"Pearlers" used to gather pearls from
oysters and trochus shells washed
onto the beach at low tide. From
about 1880, hard hat diving suits
enabled people to gather the prized
pearls from deeper water.

self Assessment

Rate your slope.

Needs work

Good effort

Best ever!

You are going on a cruise aboard a luxury ship. Fill in your boarding card.

BOARDING CARD

Passenger's Name:

Date of Birth: / /

Address – Street Number:

Street Name:

Suburb or Town:

State: Postcode:

Telephone Number:

Country of Birth

Number of brothers:

Number of sisters:

Cabin Number:

Today's Date: / /

Ticket Number:

Choose at least three of the headings below.
Write each one in a different kind of lettering.

Warning! Sharks!
How to wash a wetsuit
Surfing for fun and profit
Five years in a submersible
The day I was swallowed by a whale
Ban drift-netting!
Come to beautiful Dragon's Head Bay!

Rewrite these long words.
Lift your pencil at the touch joins. This mark ˅ will help you.

laundry backyard holiday

crowded sausages thoughtless

daughter alphabet telegraph

Mark all the pencil lifts in the words below using this mark /. The first one has been done for you. Then copy.

signature everywhere adjustment

Handwriting hints – Taking breaks in words

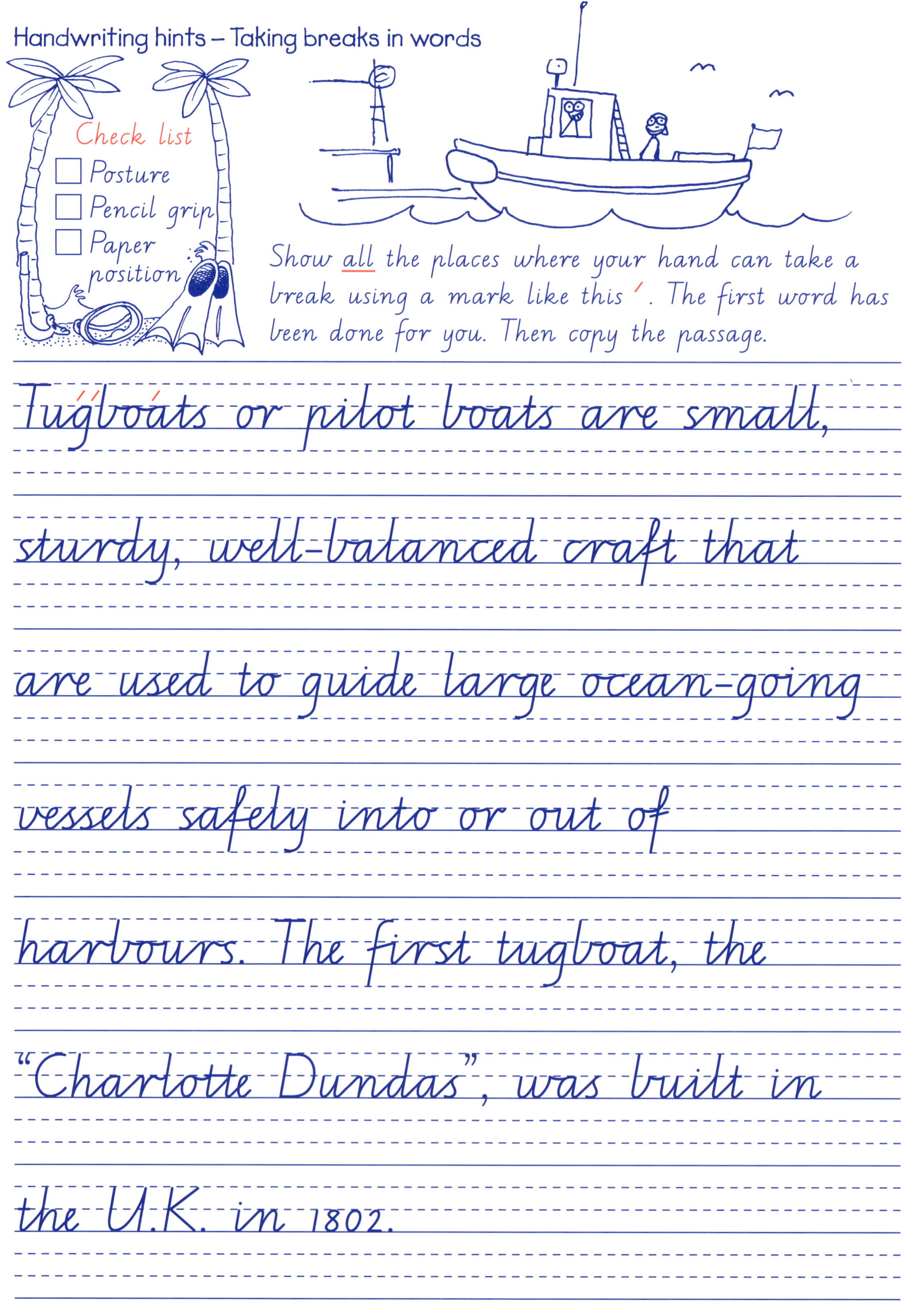

Show all the places where your hand can take a break using a mark like this ʹ. The first word has been done for you. Then copy the passage.

Tugʹboaʹts or pilot boats are small, sturdy, well-balanced craft that are used to guide large ocean-going vessels safely into or out of harbours. The first tugboat, the "Charlotte Dundas", was built in the U.K. in 1802.

Use a ruler and dot in extension lines to show the parallel letters in the words below.

Species of tuna include Little, Bigeye,

Butterfly and Yellowfin.

Copy out the text. Then dot in extension lines to see if the letters in your writing are parallel.

self Assessment

Rate your slope.

Needs work

Good effort

Best ever!

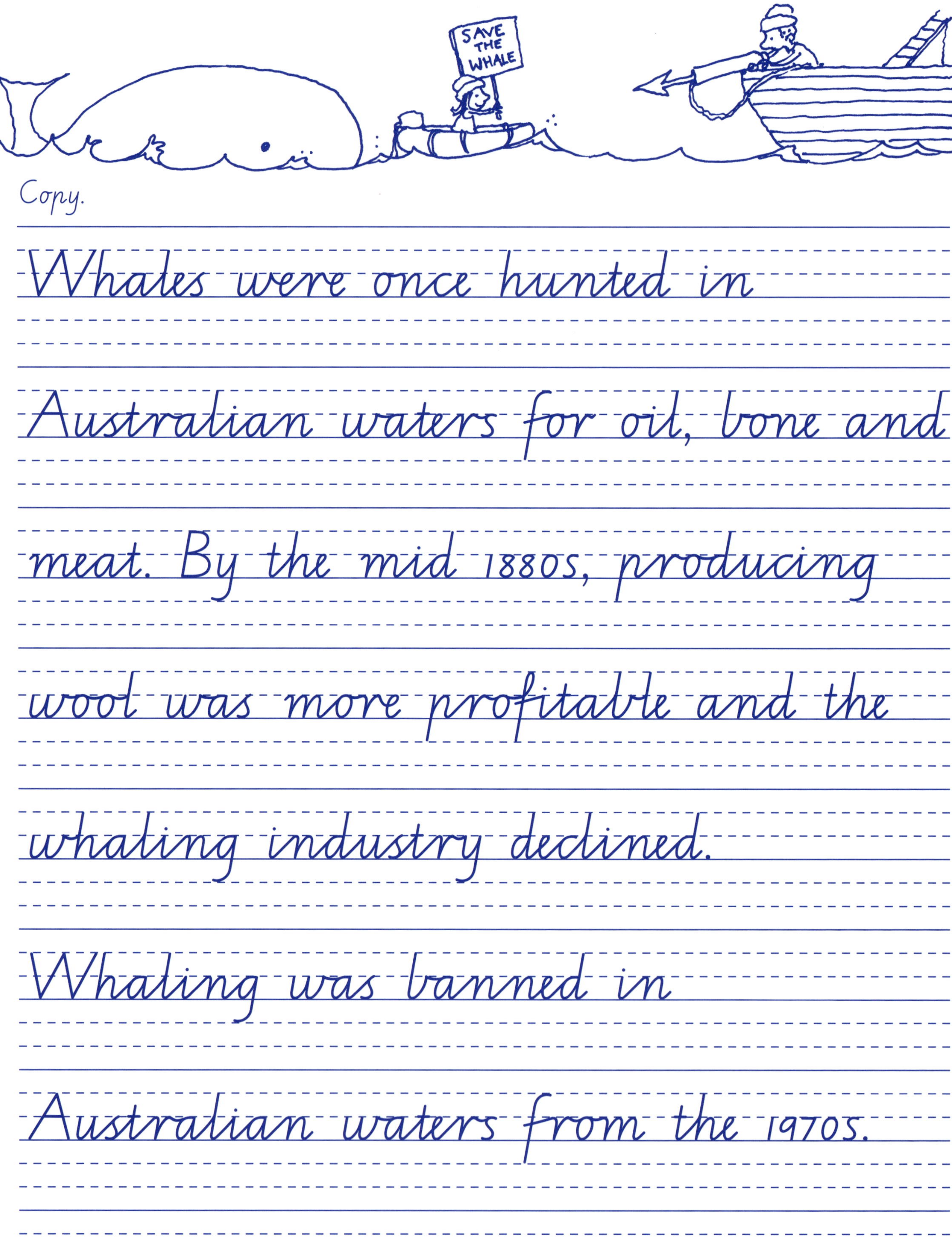

Copy.

Whales were once hunted in

Australian waters for oil, bone and

meat. By the mid 1880s, producing

wool was more profitable and the

whaling industry declined.

Whaling was banned in

Australian waters from the 1970s.

Now look at the line that contains the word "profitable". Dot in the extension lines to show the slope for each word in that line.

Put a mark ʹ above each place where you will lift your pencil. Then copy.

Humpback Whale Beaked Whale

Orca Beluga Whale Right Whale

Copy this sentence. Dot in extension lines to check your slope.

Whale watching is a popular

activity along the coast of Australia.

Write each whale-spotting area in joined writing. Pay special attention to even slope.

Hervey Bay, Qld Eden, NSW

Speed loops from descenders

You can write faster while still being neat. Make a speed loop to join from g, j, y and z.

The upstroke crosses on the line and joins to the next letter.

gi

upstroke crosses on the line

Cross out ✗ the speed loops that are too high or too low.

gi gi gi ge ge ge go go go

Trace then copy these letter pairs.

yo ya ge gi ju ja zo zi za

Trace then copy these words.

adjust pizza great anyone

Cross out ✗ the incorrect speed loops.

ja ji je je yo yo ya yu zo

Trace and copy these words with speed loops.

yoyo jeep zipper green yes

yeast bigger zinc joyous

ab ob

Trace and copy these letter pairs.

ib rk ah uk ol rb ok sh ck

wl ob el th ak sl wh ch al

Trace and copy these words with speed loops.

ribbon chicken able strife

these those that awful chalk

Cross out ✗ the incorrect speed loops.

Trace and copy these words with speed loops.

self Assessment

Circle the word with the best speed loops.

Speed loops – When not to loop

Trace and copy these letter pairs.

qu od et ip qu dr to pr qu

Speed loops are not needed when b, h, k or l are at the beginning of the word.

no speed loop

✓ land NOT land ✗

Trace and copy these words.

buying loud keep hurry

bauble lovely khaki hitch

Rewrite these letter pairs with speed loops.

gi ya ju zo gr ye jo zi

Rewrite these letter pairs with speed loops.

ub th ck pl rb oh ok el

Rewrite these words using speed loops when necessary.

misjudge buzz about hoot

duck these lying really

cheap easily grown quietly

Teacher

Before you start:

★ underline all the horizontal joins to s

★ circle all the diagonal joins to s.

Then copy.

Pearlers still dive for pearls, but
now use modern diving equipment.
Oysters are also grown in oyster
farms close to the shore, where the
pearls can be collected more easily.

Trace and copy each letter combination.
Then copy the word.

bl blend dr drover fl flower

gl gleam gr growl pl pleasant

sc science tr transport nt bent

ok look nd pretend st haste

ch chair th there scr screech

shr shriek spl splash spr spring

squ squash str straight thr thread

What would you want to have with you on a desert island?
Write a list in joined writing with speed loops. Number it from 1 to 10.

Super Challenge!

- Underline any horizontal joins to e.
- Put a tick above any diagonal joins to e.
- Circle any words with double letters.
- Put a cross under any diagonal joins to s.

Ask 10 people in your class how they like their fish cooked: battered, crumbed or grilled? Record their answers as tally marks in the box below. Use print script for the headings in your tally box.

Present the information as a bar graph. Use print script for the labels and heading of your graph.

Write a generalisation about the information you have gathered, in your best joined writing.

You are on a diving holiday in the Great Barrier Reef. Write a postcard to a friend telling them about your trip. Write the address in print script, and use joined writing for the rest.

Here is a letter written aboard a luxury ship, "The Sea Turtle". Fill in the missing letters and add the correct punctuation.

he ea urtle
23rd arch 200
ear ack
eve been on the ship he Sea urtle for 14 nights now s been great he weathers been warm and sunny e stayed in the alapagos slands for two nights Can you uess what I finally saw up close ou guessed it I saw the marine iguanas ee you soon
our friend
Jill

Did you add:

17 capital letters	yes ☐	no ☐	3 apostrophes	yes ☐	no ☐
2 sets of speech marks	yes ☐	no ☐	1 question mark	yes ☐	no ☐
2 commas	yes ☐	no ☐	2 exclamation marks	yes ☐	no ☐
5 full stops	yes ☐	no ☐			

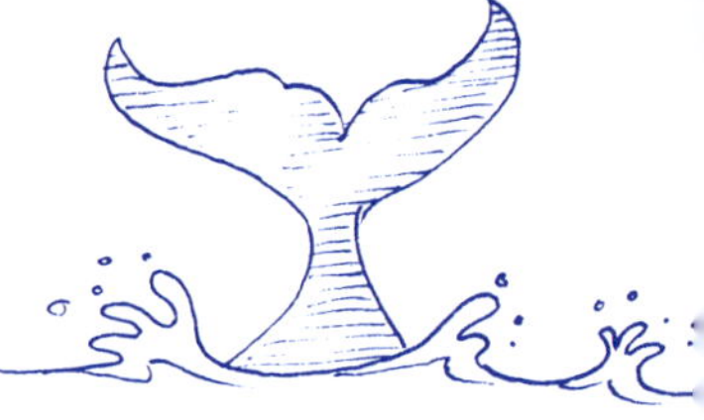

Order these whales according to size from smallest to largest. Write the whale names in joined writing.

Orca or Killer Whale — 8 m	Sperm Whale — 17 m
Blue Whale — 30 m	Narwhal — 4.9 m + tooth 2-3 m
Southern Right Whale — 16 m	Minke Whale — 10 m
Humpback Whale — 14 m	Beluga Whale — 4.6 m
Bowhead Whale — 15 m	Pilot Whale — 5-7 m

self Assessment

Check your slope by dotting in extension lines. Rate your slope.

Needs work

Good effort

Best ever!

These are word pictures. Word pictures are fun to do and can be useful as headings. Make a word picture for each of these words, then do two of your own.

diving wave

Imagine you are a surf lifesaver. Write about a day in your life. Start by writing a rough draft on another piece of paper. Write your final draft here in joined writing, as neatly as you can. Add a heading and a border.